# Quiz Number 1

1. Who has an allergic reaction to Monica's Kiwi lime pie?
2. Which member of the group has a third nipple?
3. What type of animal is 'Hugsy'?
4. How does it end when Ross try's to move his new sofa to his apartment?
5. what is the name of the game show that Joey appears on and looses almost every round?
6. Before going on a date with Monica's work colleague Hillary, what does Ross do to his teeth?
7. In season 8 what does Ross dress as for Halloween?
8. In season one episode nine, why is Monica's Thanksgiving food ruined?
9. What animal does Phoebe find in her guitar case in season four?
10. What does Phoebe initially change her name to when she gets married?

# QUIZ NUMBER 2

1. What happens after Rachel try's out walking around the apartment naked.
2. Why doesn't Rachel want Ross to take Emma on the swings?
3. Who do Monica and Chandler find watching them have sex when they are trying to conceive a child?
4. What is the name of the birth mother of the child Monica and Chandler have been put forward to adopt?
5. Why does Chandler start smoking again in season three?
6. Who does Ross tell that he did not annul his and Rachel's Vegas marriage?
7. What activity do Phoebe and Rachel do to try and bond together?
8. When everyone wants to leave Emma's first birthday party how do the gang decide who has to stay and who gets to leave?
9. Who does Phoebe give her 'Gladys' (a three-dimensional painting of a half-bald mannequin) to?
10. When Rachel's department at Bloomingdale's closes she gets demoted to which position?

# The One With All The Questions

## A Friends Quiz Book

### Unofficial & Unauthorised

### Erica Moss

greenthumbpublishing@gmail.com

# QUIZZES

# Quiz Number 3

1. While in a job interview Chandler finds it hard to not make a joke when his potential employer uses which word?
2. When Chandler wants to help Monica make Thanksgiving dinner what does she put him in charge of making?
3. Why does Chandler want to swap shoes with Joey at his wedding reception?
4. What do bob and Faye Bing send Chandler that hates but Monica insists they keep incase they visit?
5. Did Ross go into Bonnie or Rachel's room at the end of season three?
6. After forgetting to make Chandler a homemade gift for Valentine's day what does Monica give Chandler?
7. What is the name of Joey's girlfriend who keeps punching him on the arm?
8. What is the name of Ross and Monica's parents friend that Monica ends up dating in season two?
9. What do Monica and Ross do to try get on TV at new years?
10. Why do Joey and Chandler end up swapping apartments with Rachel and Monica?

# QUIZ NUMBER 4

1. Who does Jeff Goldblum make a cameo appearance as in season 9?
2. How do Rachel and Phoebe find out about Monica and Chandler?
3. Where do Ross and Rachel have their first kiss?
4. In season 9 how much was the jackpot for the state lottery?
5. What character does Ross create to teach Ben about Hanukkah?
6. In the first episode of season two, who cuts the hair of both Monica and Julie?
7. What is the name of Joey's sister that comes to Rachel for advice when she get pregnant?
8. When his children are four years old, Phoebe's half-brother Frank Jr. brings his children to visit Phoebe, what is his intention on this trip?
9. Who do Phoebe and Monica forget to invite to Rachel's baby shower?
10. Although not wanting to get married in Vegas, Monica and Chandler still want to take their relationship to the next level. How do they intend to do this?

# Quiz Number 5

1. While Phoebe is working as a telephone sales woman what is the name of the man she speaks to who wants to commit suicide?
2. What is the name of the manager of Central Perk coffeeshop?
3. When Ross starts dating Cheryl, who everyone agrees is beautiful, Rachel notices one flaw with her. What was her flaw?
4. What type of car does Joey find the keys to?
5. What does Ross find out about the Paleontology section in the library that makes him guard it?
6. When Chandler is moving in with Monica and Rachel is moving out what is the name of Joey's new room mate?
7. What is the name of the female co-creator of Friends?
8. Who is in the bath when Ross and Rachel tell the gang they're having a baby girl?
9. While driving back from Vegas who accompanies Joey?
10. What is the name of Phoebes dad?

# QUIZ NUMBER 6

1.  What is the name of the diner that Monica takes a job at after loosing the last of her savings on stocks?

2.  What is the name of Ross's student that asks him on a date?

3.  What does piece of furniture Monica not want Chandler to bring into their apartment ?

4.  Who witnessed Ben's first word?

5.  Why does Ross get given a ticket by Officer Petty?

6.  During a date Ross cannot put back on a pair of leather pants he purchased, who does he call for advice?

7.  How does Joey's character in 'Days of Our Lives' die?

8.  What ceramic animal does Joey give to Chandler before he moves out?

9.  What are the names of the couple that Monica and Chandler met on their honeymoon and loved?

10. Who asks Ross to nap with him but he finds it too weird?

# Quiz Number 7

1. What is the name of the gangs favorite coffeeshop?
2. In season 5 why does Phoebe give her coat away to a stranger?
3. While hanging out in Central Perk, Chandler sees a girl and decides to ask her out. She turns out to Joey's date, what is her name?
4. Towards the end of season three Chandlers new boss has a unusual way of praising his employees. What did he do?
5. What does Monica decide to do to help her get over Richard near the start of season three?
6. What is Joey's infamous pickup line?
7. Why do Chandler and Monica fight on their first anniversary?
8. Who do Carol and Susan use as their wedding caterer after the original caterer gets into an accident?
9. What does Rachel buy for $1,000 and sell to Gunther for $1,500?
10. After being initially depressed about his break up with Kathy, Chandler wants to go to a strip club, who does he go with?

# QUIZ NUMBER 8

1. What is the last line of the last episode?
2. Why does Monica almost resign from her position as head chef in season four?
3. What is Gunther referring to when he says 'Hey buddy, this is a family place. Put the mouse back in the house!'?
4. What did Gunther do before becoming awaiter?
5. What is the name of the hot nanny Ross and Rachel hire that Joey goes crazy for?
6. In light of his recent eviction and impending divorce, what happens at work to finally break Ross?
7. Why is Phoebe unhappy that her brother Frank Jr. is marrying Alice?
8. When Rachel is pregnant and Joey takes her on a date, what is the name of the horror movie they watched on the date?
9. Why does Ross sell all his furniture after Emily moves in with him?
10. Why does Chandler start smoking inOklahoma?

# Quiz Number 9

1. What is the name of the magazine that Joey is being interviewed for in season 8?

2. What does Phoebe give to Monica as an engagement present?

3. Why dos Gunther threaten to fire Joey from his job at central perk?

4. When the cake is picked up from the bakery what shape is the cake at Emma's first birthday party?

5. In season 8 why does Rachel's date with Joey's co-worker Kash go badly?

6. Where does Chandler tell Janice he has been relocated to avoid her?

7. Which band do Ross, Monica and Chandler go to see for Ross' birthday?

8. What name of Rachel and Ross's Daughter?

9. Who does Phoebe ask to walk her down the isle after her father can no longer do it?

10. How does Joey choose to punish Chandler for Kissing Kathy?

# Quiz Number 10

1. What is the name of Monica's aunt who is a professional poker player?
2. Who does Chandler accidentally see topless after taking a shower in season one?
3. Where does Monica work after leaving Allesandro's?
4. Why is Phoebes father unable to make it to her wedding to walk her down the isle?
5. What happened to Monica's downstairs neighbor when he stopped knocking to tell them to quieten down?
6. What is the name of the game show that Joey auditions to be the host of?
7. At Chandler's work Christmas he and Monica are invited by Chandler's boss to play which sport?
8. Who is Phoebe surprised to meet at her Grandmothers funeral?
9. After a power outage Chandler finds himself trapped in an ATM vestibule with which Victoria Secret's model?
10. What is the name of the male nanny that Ross is uncomfortable with?

# QUIZ NUMBER 11

1. What mistake does Ross make while saying his vows to Emily?
2. After being told that Marcel got sick and died Ross is surprised to be told that Marcel had not died. What was the real reason Marcel wasn't at the zoo?
3. What does Joey buy Chandler and Monica as a house warming present?
4. What TV show does Joey's grandmother want to see him on?
5. After Ross and Rachel breakup in season three Ross acts out of spite and asks for a specific item of clothing back. What is this item of clothing?
6. Which member of the group helps out Joey by plucking his eyebrows?
7. What is the first wedding present Monica opens while waiting for Chandler to come home?
8. Where does Chandlers father live?
9. Where does Rachel work after leaving her job at Forunata Fashions?
10. Who played Chandler Bing?

# Quiz Number 12

1. What does Ross use to try to bribe Ugly Naked Guy into giving him his apartment?
2. Who played Joey Tribbiani?
3. Why do the gang take a trip to Montauk after Phoebe finds a photo with her mother writing on the back?
4. What was the name of the comic Ross made when he was a kid?
5. What color sweater does Rachel buy for Ross after he asks for fashion advice for a date he's going to go on?
6. Who dated 'The Screamer', 'The Yeti' and the man with the 'Inappropriate Sister'?
7. After seeing the seating plan to his and Monica's wedding why does Chandler get upset?
8. What is the name of Ross and Monica's aunt who they hate?
9. What is Rachel talking about when she shouts "Just so you know, it's NOT that common, it DOESN'T happen to every guy and it IS a big deal!" at Ross?
10. When Ross leaves Ben with Monica and Rachel what happens that Ross is annoyed about?

# Quiz Number 13

1. In season 4 who does Joey go on a fishing trip with?
2. Why does Phoebe get fired from her job as a masseuse?
3. During one Thanksgiving what is Joey trying to do when he gets a turkey stuck on his head?
4. Why are Ross and Joey late for the thanksgiving meal Chandler and Monica made?
5. After Phoebe and Mike exchange apartment keys, which of Phoebes ex-boyfriends shows up that she then kisses?
6. What activity do Phoebe and Rachel do to try and bond together?
7. On the TV show called Mac & C.H.E.E.S.E. that Joey is auditioning for what is the name of character he is auditioning for?
8. What does Ross and Monica's father give to Monica to prove he loves her as much as Ross?
9. Who teaches Emma to hold up a finger to show how old she is?
10. Why do Rachel and Joey end up breakingup?

# Quiz Number 14

1. What does Rachel buy Chandler in season three to try to get him to stop smoking?
2. After Rachel looses Marcel the monkey where do Phoebe and Monica find him?
3. What can't Chandler do that causes Joey to say he's 'dead inside.'?
4. Why in season 6 do Phoebe and Rachel brag about being able to kick anyone's ass?
5. What is the name of Monica and Chandlers relator?
6. When one of Mike's groomsmen can't make it to the wedding who does mike decide should replace him?
7. After forgetting to make Monica a homemade gift for Valentine's day what does Chandler give Monica?
8. Chandlers co-worker Bob always misnames him, what does he call him?
9. Towards the end of season three Ross has a mysterious skin condition, what area of his body did the skin condition affect?
10. Who accompanies Rachel to visit her father after he's suffered a heart attack?

# QUIZ NUMBER 15

1. Why is Ross scared when Emily offers to accompany Susan on a trip to London?
2. What is the name of Charlie's ex-boyfriend who is still in love with her?
3. Why does Joey say to Chandler that that Monica is getting a boob job?
4. What do Frank and Alice ask for from Phoebe as a present after they get married?
5. What made Emma laugh for the first time?
6. Who wrote the song titled 'Smelly Cat'?
7. What is the name of the vice president of the Oklahoma branch that try's to seduce Chandler at Christmas?
8. What surrounds the peep-hole on the door of Monica's apartment?
9. When Ross thinks he has started dating a woman called Amanda she is actually using him for what?
10. When Ross joins his collage alumni site what does Chandler first write on Ross's page?

# Quiz Number 16

1. What is the problem with the "stripper" Monica hires for Chandlers bachelor party?
2. What is the name of the first fashion company Rachel gets a job at?
3. What museum did Ross work at?
4. What does Ross catch Paul doing at Elizabeth's grandmothers cottage?
5. How does Phoebe stop Rachels plane from taking off?
6. What is the name of the area that Monica and Chandler plan on moving to after they adopt?
7. While clearing out Mr. Heckles apartment, Ross finds something of interest to him, what does he find?
8. Where did Ross end up when he fell asleep on the train in "The One With The Girl From Poughkeepsie"?
9. How many years have Ross and Monica's parents been married when they let Monica give the speech at the anniversary celebration?
10. Before Rachel leaves for Paris what stops Ross for confessing his love to Rachel in central perk?

# Quiz Number 17

1. Why do Richard and Monica break up?
2. How does Joey's character in 'Days of Our Lives' make a comeback?
3. How does Joey try to frame Ross for breaking his fridge?
4. When going to the Premiere of Joey's new play Ross surprises Rachel by announcing that he is bringing a date. In retaliation Rachel also brings a date. What was the name of Rachels date?
5. During season two Chandler and Joey are attempting to look after Ben while Ross is in hospital. They don't do a great job and end up loosing him. Where do they leave him?
6. What do chandler and Monica name theirson?
7. What does Phoebe try to help Joey learn for an audition in season 10?
8. After watching the start of the tape of Ross and Rachel hooking up who do the group agree initiated the sex?
9. What is the name of, Phoebe's boyfriend, Mike's father?
10. Which member of the group kisses Chandlers mom in season one?

# Quiz Number 18

1. What is the problem with the job Rachel gets offered at Louis Vuitton?
2. What is the name of the dog that Phoebe gets Joey to cheer him up?
3. When Phoebe is short for cash how does Joey help her find her a job?
4. What is the name of Ross' new girlfriend during the start of season two?
5. When Chandler starts to put on some unwanted weight in season two who does he ask to be his personal trainer to help him loose the weight?
6. What language does Marcel the monkey change the TV to in season one?
7. What is the name of Rachels boyfriend who everyone says in a identical copy of Ross?
8. What is the name of the man who stalks Phoebe thinking that she is Ursula?
9. Who marries Phoebe and Mike?
10. Why promise does Chandler make to Phoebe so that she pays him $7,000?

# Quiz Number 19

1. What is Chandler's middle name?
2. Why does Paul tell Ross he isn't allow to see Elizabeth anymore?
3. Who helped Phoebe plan her wedding?
4. What is the name of Monica's sous-chef that Phoebe has a crush on in season 8 ?
5. Who gets stung by a jellyfish in the first episode of the fourth season?
6. What fear does Rachels boyfriend Joshua have in season 4?
7. What name does Phoebe choose for Frank and Alice's third child?
8. When Ross and Rachel lock themselves out of their apartment with Emma still inside, who are they waiting for to open the door?
9. In season 6 what does Phoebe's psychic predict will happen to her?
10. What is the name of Monica's alcoholic boyfriend who his only funny when he drinks?

# Quiz Number 20

1. Who impersonated Joey's agent Estelle on the phone to him after her death?
2. On Halloween who wins the arm wrestle between Ross and Chandler?
3. When Joey moves out in season two, who ends up keeping the foosball table?
4. Whose catchphrase is 'Oh My God!'?
5. In what season does Rachel turn 30?
6. What is the name of the guy that Rachel gives her phone number too after she's had Emma and is ready to start dating again?
7. When Monica surprises Chandler at his hotel in Tulsa, what does Chandler hide that he's watching?
8. When Chandler is moving in with Monica and Rachel is moving out what do Rachel and Monica fight over, both claiming they own?
9. What is the name of the wedding dress shop Monica visits that has a 50% sale on?
10. Who played Phoebe Buffay?

# Quiz Number 21

1. After Joey and Chandlers table breaks they cannot agree on a new table, they are debating between a table with a bird-pattern and a ladybug-pattern. But which table do they go for in the end?

2. What was the name of the club that Ross and his friend Will created about Rachel while they were all at school together?

3. Where do Phoebe and Mike get married?

4. What is the name of Chandlers new room mate who moves in after Joey moves out?

5. What does Joy buy for his and Chandlers apartment after his success in the TV show Days of Our Lives?

6. In season 9 where is Ross's conference that everyone travels to held?

7. When Joey and Monica take an 'introduction to cooking class' what does Joey make that is better than Monica's?

8. Why does someone recognize Phoebe and ask for her autograph?

9. In 'The one with the lottery', what causes Phoebe to drop the bowl of tickets?

10. Who wakes up baby Emma causing her to not stop crying?

# Quiz Number 22

1. How does Rachel try to bond with her new employees at Ralph Lauren?

2. What do Ross and Rachel do on their first date?

3. During season one, Phoebe offers to break up with her boyfriend Tony to make it easier for Chandler to break up with who?

4. Who is the youngest Friend?

5. What is the name of the man Phoebe married to allow him to get a green card to stay living in the U.S. ?

6. What part of New York is Rachel originally from?

7. How does Joey make everyone cry at Emma's first birthday party?

8. Who does Joey hold a funeral service for after they die?

9. In season one episode two, what does Rachel loose in Monica's Lasagna

10. What does Joey initially suggest to Ross as Chandlers punishment for Kissing Kathy, that Ross talks him out of?

# Quiz Number 23

1. On the way to Rachel's sisters cabin, while stopping at a restroom, Rachel locks the car keys in the car. How do the gang solve this problem ?
2. How many women give birth before Rachel in the hospital (i.e. the same day)?
3. What is Rachel's father's occupation?
4. What do Phoebe and Monica buy to support their catering business in season four?
5. Who pee's on Monica in season four in order to ease the pain of her jellyfish sting?
6. Who does Rachel go on a date with after splitting up with Ross to get back at him?
7. Who does Rachel find out that Mindy, her best friend, is marrying?
8. Which of Joey's sisters does Chandler grope at his birthday party?
9. Why is Ross suspended from his job at the museum?
10. How many children does Phoebe have for Alice and Frank?

# Quiz Number 24

1. What instrument does Ross initially propose to play at Monica and Chandlers wedding?
2. When Emily agrees to move to New York to work on her and Ross's relationship, what does she ask Ross to stop doing?
3. What is the name of Rosses lesbian ex-wife?
4. Who convinces Rachel to get a tattoo of a heart on her hip?
5. What is the name of building superintendent at Monica, Rachel, Joey and Chandlers apartment building?
6. After being promoted at Ralph Lauren in season 7 what can Rachel now do?
7. Why does Phoebe gift Joey a drum kit and tarantula?
8. What is the name of the employee at Chandlers gym that both he and Ross find attractive?
9. Ross and Mona take a picture of themselves together and Mona wants to send it to everyone as a holiday card, where was this photo taken?
10. What is the synthetic chocolate substitute that Monica has to use to create a number of recipes for a job interview in season two?

# Quiz Number 25

1.  In season 6 everyone is thinking about what could have been in a parellel universe, what does Phoebe think about?
2.  What is the name of Phoebe's twin sister?
3.  Why does Joey get his Ministers license?
4.  After being fired from Ralph Lauren what company does Rachel get offered a job at by Mark, who she previously dated?
5.  After getting offered a job at Ralph Lauren what does Rachel accidentally do to her interviewer instead of shaking his hand?
6.  After going on a date with Phoebe's friend Sarah in season 10 why does Joey not call her back?
7.  Why is Phoebe not happy with the stripper at her bachelorette party?
8.  What character does George Clooney make a cameo appearance as in season one?
9.  Where does Chandler accidentally accept to move him and Monica to for work?
10. What is the name of Phoebes half-brother?

# QUIZ NUMBER 26

1. After clearing out Monica's bedroom to start converting it into a gym her parents drop her a box containing a video tape of a significant event. What was on the video tape?

2. What is the name of Joey's character on 'Days Of Our Lives'?

3. What zoo does Marcel the monkey get accepted into?

4. Why did Monica say Rachel stole her thunder on the day she got engaged?

5. Monica is upset that Richard Burke has nothing that he Is obsessed about, until she finds out that he is obsessed with one thing. What is he obsessed with?

6. Who played Rachel Green?

7. Who tells Rachel that Ross slept with Chloe after they had a fight on their anniversary?

8. When Joey and Chandler go to Richards apartment to view it for potential purchase, what do they find?

9. Why in the fourth season do Rachel and Monica almost get kicked out of their apartment?

10. After the death of the Monica and Ross' aunt Monica inherits an item that she always wanted during her childhood. What was this item?

# Quiz Number 27

1. What happens on Ross and Rachels first anniversary?
2. Why does Rachel end up making a half trifle, half shepherds pie, on thanksgiving?
3. What is the name of Joey's favorite stuffed animal?
4. When meeting Chandler for the first time, everyone except one member of the group thought he was gay. Who thought Chandler wasn't gay?
5. Towards the end of season three Phoebe starts dating two guys at the same time. What was the name of the firefighter she was seeing?
6. What does Eddie do while Chandler is asleep that makes him uncomfortable?
7. in season 6 Joey initially try's to hide where he is working from his friends, where was he working?
8. What is the name of Phoebes ex-singingpartner?
9. What is the name of Ross' son?
10. What is the name of the bakery that accidentally deliver the 'best cheesecake ever' to Chandlers flat?

# QUIZ NUMBER 28

1. How did ross and Chandler originally know each other?
2. What message does Phoebe read in her own tea leaves In season 8?
3. Where does David (Phoebe's boyfriend) move to?
4. What excuse does Phoebe make for Ross after he says Emily during his wedding ceremony?
5. Who gets married in Vegas on Monica and Chandlers first anniversary?
6. What is the name of the male co-creator of Friends?
7. What is the name of Ross' girlfriend who goes to Montauk with the gang in the season three finale?
8. During season 4 Joey gets a job with Ross at the museum he works at. What is his job role?
9. What is the name of Joey's acting agent?
10. Who was Monica's first kiss?

# Quiz Number 29

1. What is the name of the professor that Ross brings to Joeys Days of Our Lives party?
2. Joey is the face of a sexually transmitted disease poster campaign, this causes his family as well as a number of women to believe that he actually has the disease. What disease was this?
3. What impresses Phoebe about the health inspector that she beings dating?
4. Joey's acting agent manages to get him a job as a 'butt double' for which famous actor?
5. What is the name of the guy Phoebe is dating, who is a foreign diplomat from 'Ichnech Traian Istan'?
6. What is Ross' favorite song?
7. Why does Monica get applauded at Mike's karaoke night despite not being a great singer?
8. How many episodes of Friends were there?
9. What is the name of Rachels sister who she accidentally convinces to ask Ross on a date?
10. What TV channel do Joey and Chandler find that makes them never turn off their TV in fear the channel will disappear?

# Quiz Number 30

1. What does know that Monica and Chandler did that he wont tell Rachel and Ross if they name their first born child Joey?

2. Who played Monica Geller?

3. At Ross and Emily's wedding reception what stops Monica and Chandler from having sex in the Wine cellar?

4. Why are Monica and Ross resistant to playing a gave football on thanksgiving in season three?

5. What lead up to Ross accidentally recording him and Rachel hooking up?

6. In season four who does Monica invite to Thanksgiving?

7. Who does Ross take inspiration from when getting a spray tan?

8. Who was the most credited director in the Friends series?

9. Why do Chandler and Kathy break up?

10. When getting seated for the Premiere of Joey's new play Rachels date does something to shock Ross. What did he do?

# QUIZ NUMBER 31

1. What is Emma's first word?
2. When Joey has a dream about Rachel and Ross's baby, what's strange about the baby?
3. At the end of which season do Monica and Chandler get engaged?
4. Who gets baby Emma's ears pierced?
5. When Monica is made Head Chef of a restaurant in season four she hires another member of the gang as a waiter. Who does she hire?
6. Where do Ross and Carol get inspiration for their sons name?
7. Who writes Monica and Chandlers letter of recommendation for adoption?
8. What is the name of Phoebe and Monica's old roommate that comes to visit in season 10?
9. After getting stuck on the roof while looking for a comet, how do Joey and Ross escape?
10. When helping Monica pack Joey and Ross find a pair of handcuffs, who do they belong to?

# QUIZ NUMBER 32

1. Who, from Ralph Lauren, does Rachel set Chandler up on a date with in season three?
2. When Rachel drags Chandler to the nail studio who does he bump into?
3. Where do Chick Jr. and Duck Jr. get stuck?
4. How does Emily respond when Ross expresses his love to her at the airport?
5. In season four why does Chandler do after confessing to Joey that he kissed Kathy?
6. How many siblings does Chandler have?
7. What sort of company does Chandler intern at after leaving his job in Oklahoma?
8. Why does Phoebe hate PBS?
9. What does Ross walk in on Rachel doing with Elizabeth's father?
10. Where do Ross and Chandler go when Ross gets high on candy?

# Quiz Number 33

1. What is the name of the guy who Phoebe thinks is Monica's soul-mate? Allesandro's is one of his favorite restaurants and they both want to live in a house made of cheese.
2. Why was Monica not invited to her and Ross's cousins wedding?
3. What competition does Phoebe want to enter Emma into?
4. In season four who's apartment gets robbed?
5. Ross sends a joke into which magazine that ends up getting printed?
6. Monica finds what she believes to be a useless switch in her apartment. What does this switch do?
7. When Joey agrees to read Rachels book recommendation 'Little Women', what does Joey ask Rachel to read?
8. What was the fire in Phoebes apartment caused by?
9. When Judy arrives at the hospital before Rachel gives birth she brings a ring to give to Ross, who's ring was this originally?
10. When Joey has to kiss a guy as part of an acting job who ends up kissing Joey to practice?

# QUIZ NUMBER 34

1. Why did Chandler hide the fact he is a really good table tennis player?
2. When everyone thinks Chandler is cheating on Monica what is really going on?
3. What ruins Chandlers plans to propose to Monica at the restaurant?
4. After enrolling in a medical experiment why do Joey and his friend Carl get turned away?
5. Who did Ross loose his virginity too?
6. What does Ross say he wont do until he names all 50 states?
7. Where do Monica and Chandler go to meet the potential birth mother of the child they may be adopting?
8. What is the name of the guy Chandler and Ross know who was nicknamed 'Hums While He Pees guy' that Phoebe dates?
9. When talking to Bill and Colleen about adoption Chandler accidentally tell's Owen something he didn't already know, what was this?
10. What is the nickname of the nudist who lives across from Monica and Rachel?

# QUIZ NUMBER 35

1. Who teaches Phoebe how to ride a bike?
2. Towards the end of season three Phoebe starts dating two guys at the same time. What was the name of the teacher she was seeing?
3. What was the occupation of Rachel's ex-fiancé Barry?
4. Why is Ross scared to date one of his students, Elizabeth?
5. How does Rachels bosses find out that her and Tag are seeing each other?
6. What is the name of Chandlers cousin that he hires a stripper for during season three?
7. Why does Phoebe not like going to thedentist?
8. What is the name of Ross and Rachels Pediatrician that dropped them?
9. After their first date Ross and Rachel kiss, but what does Ross do to make Rachel burst into laughter?
10. What causes Rachel's water to break?

# Quiz Number 36

1. What hair style does Monica adopt in an attempt to get rid of her poofy hair?

2. Phoebe has to stop massaging Monica, why is this?

3. While taking a nap in Rachel's bed what does Joey find out that Rachel does in her alone time?

4. Why does Chandler lie to the group and tell them that he is allergic to dogs?

5. What is 'the giant poking device' madefrom?

6. When Joey and Phoebe set up Ross and Rachel with terrible blind dates Joey cancels Ross's date without telling him, but what's wrong with Rachel's date?

7. Why does Ross try to get Ben interested in GI Joe and dinosaurs in season three?

8. What is the name of Rachel's boss at Ralph Lauren?

9. When everyone returns from the wedding in London the gang plan a trip to Atlantic city. What stops them from going?

10. What is the name of the musician that's son is in the same school class as Ben?

# Quiz Number 37

1. Why does Joshua initially say that he cannot date Rachel?
2. While Phoebe is dreaming Ross say's something to annoy her, what did he say in the dream?
3. Ross get's a pager so that he can be notified when Carol goes into labor. What is the number of this pager?
4. What animal does Joey adopt in season three after watching a news article?
5. Why does Ross and Monica's friend from school, named Will Colbert, hate Rachel?
6. What is Chandler's mother's job?
7. Joey is freaked out when he see's Ginger, one of his ex-girlfriends. They split up after he accidentally threw something of hers in the fireplace. What was this item?
8. After giving a homeless person $1000, Phoebe buys a soda and it contains a strange and disgusting item. What did Phoebe find?
9. What does Phoebe name the rat in her flat that mike kills?
10. Where are Chandler and Monica planning on going on holiday shortly after Emma's first birthday?

# Quiz Number 38

1. What is the name of Rachel's dad?
2. What company is Rachel being interviewed for when she sees her current employer in the same restaurant as her interview?
3. On the TV show called Mac & C.H.E.E.S.E. what does C.H.E.E.S.E. stand for?
4. When Joey and Ross end up dating the same girl Kirsten without knowing, how do they decide to settle who gets to keep dating her?
5. Who played Ross Geller?
6. What does Ross write on a fake collage alumni page for Chandler?
7. What is the name of Joey's chair that Rachel breaks?
8. After giving up learning to sail Joey decides to enjoy sailing his own way, how does he do this?
9. What is the name of the girl that Mike is cheating on Phoebe with and Phoebe breaks up with her on his behalf?
10. To what sports event does Mike take Phoebe to in hopes of proposing to her?

# QUIZ NUMBER 39

1. When Ross and Chandler made a pro's and con's list about Rachel what point annoyed her the most?

2. What language other than English is Gunther fluent in?

3. Why isn't Rachel sad when Monica and Chandler tell her that they want her to moveout?

4. during season two episode two who does Monica go shopping and then for lunch with that annoys Rachel?

5. What is the name of Joey's mother?

6. When Gary takes Ross, Chandler and Joey on a ride-along in his police car what does Gary tell Joey he's not allowed to do?

7. What is the name of the software engineer millionaire that asks out Monica while she is working at the Moon dance diner?

8. Where does Mike hide the ring that he plans to propose to Phoebe with when they're at a restaurant?

9. After throwing her fire alarm down the garbage chute who returns it to Phoebe?

10. What is the name of Rosses lesbian ex-wife's partner she met at the gym?

# QUIZ NUMBER 40

1. After Monica orders him to change from his world war one costume Joey bought a different outfit, what was this outfit?

2. What does Mike change his name to when he gets married in protest of Phoebes name?

3. What goes wrong when Phoebe is dressed as an elf and collecting money for charity?

4. During which season does Rachel quit her job at the coffee shop?

5. What goes wrong just before Monica and Chandler are going to make a homemade porn video?

6. While sitting on the roof looking for a comet what does Joey try t use as a telescope?

7. In season one of Friends, Ross has a date planned and asks another member of the group for advice in dirty talk. Who does he ask?

8. According to Ross's collage alumni site how did Ross die?

9. When Rachel is going back to work after having Emma what is the name of the person who has temporarily replaced her?

10. What is the name of the award Joey thinks he has been nominated for his comeback in Days of Our Lives?

# QUIZ NUMBER 41

1.  What is the name of the restaurant that Monica gets a job at as head chef as during season four?
2.  How do the gang end up deciding who will be Monica's maid of honor?
3.  How does Joey's character in 'Days of Our Lives' come out of a coma?
4.  How do Rachel and Monica originally know each other?
5.  What is the name of the maid that Monica thinks has stolen her jeans?
6.  Where do Ross and Phoebe get stuck before Ben is born?
7.  Near the end of season three what character decides to compete in an Ultimate Fighting Championship?
8.  During season four Joey is convinced to buy what set of books by a door to door salesman?
9.  How many seasons of Friends were there?
10. On Marcel's set Chandler meets his make-up artist Susie, they begin dating and he finds that she is very sexually aggressive. One night she asks Chandler to do something with her underwear during a date. What did she ask him to do?

# Quiz Number 42

1.  Where does Rachel work  for the first few seasons of Friends?

2.  After agreeing to let Joey be the Minister of himself and Monica's marriage, he later wants someone else to marry them, why?

3.  When Chandler and Monica go away for a romantic weekend in season 5 why do they change hotel room a number of times?

4.  Why does Phoebe not travel to London for Ross's Wedding?

5.  What is the name of Monica's coworker that she kisses while working at the Moon dance Diner?

6.  When Joey wants to look sharp before an audition he purchases a hat which everyone makes fun of, what type of hat is it?

7.  Where in New York is the gangs favorite coffeeshop located?

8.  What is Monica nervous to use the Thanksgiving after her marriage?

9.  While Phoebe is giving birth Joey believes he is having 'sympathy pains'. What do these turn out to be?

10. While watching TV in season 9 on thanksgiving where does Joey realize he's supposed to be?

# Quiz Number 43

1. What is Phoebe's late wedding present to Monica and Chandler?
2. What is the name of Chandler and Monica's pet duck and chicken they get from Joey?
3. When did the first episode of Friends air?
4. In season four why doesn't Rachel get the promotion after Joanna offers her the job?
5. When auditioning for the part of a Catholic Italian immigrant Joey has to pretend to be uncircumcised, how does he go about this?
6. Who does Ross call and complain when he finds out Rachel is pregnant with hist child?
7. When did the last episode of Friends air?
8. After a trip to Japan Monica's boyfriend Pete returns to give Monica some big news. What is this news?
9. Who does Chandler sleep with the night before Valentine's Day in season one?
10. When Monica says she won't cook a turkey for thanksgiving and Joey says he'll eat the whole thing, what is her reason not wanting to cook the turkey?

# Quiz Number 44

1. What does Ross tell Rachel is his secretfantasy?
2. What is the name of Phoebes' street friend that mugged Ross?
3. What is Chandler afraid of, causing him to run away, of just before his wedding?
4. For the first Halloween after they marry Monica try's to get Chandler a costume relating to the name of his favorite children's book, what is the name of this book?
5. What is wrong with the picture that Monica and Chandler get taken for a local news paper after getting engaged?
6. In the finale of season one what does Rachel see Ross do before boarding his plane?
7. What is the name of Rachels first personal assistant she hires at Ralph Lauren?
8. What is the name of the band Chandler wants to play at his and Monica's wedding?
9. What is the name of the social worker that visits Chandler and Monica while determining if they are good candidates to adopt a child?
10. After Joey and his new room mate Janine go on a double date with Monica and Chandler how does she describe Monica?

# QUIZ NUMBER 45

1.  What do Chandler and Monica name their daughter?
2.  What is the first item Rachel buys from pottery barn for Phoebe?
3.  Who lives in the apartment below Monica and Rachels in the early seasons?
4.  Who is the first person to make baby Emma laugh?
5.  What does Monica give to the neighbors for free that later has people queueing outside the apartment?
6.  How did Phoebes mum die?
7.  What was the name of Ross's pet monkey in season one of Friends?
8.  What is the name of the card game Chandler creates to make Joey win $1500?
9.  Who is able to turn of the heating at Christmas after Ross breaks the temperature control knob?
10. What do Mike and Phoebe do with their wedding funds?

# ANSWERS

# Quiz Number 1
## Answers

1. Ross.
2. Chandler.
3. Penguin.
4. He ends up breaking the sofa in half.
5. Pyramid.
6. He whitens them too much.
7. "Spud-nik" a mix between the Russian satellite and a potato.
8. As the gang get locked outside on the apartment balcony while the food is in the oven.
9. a cat.
10. Princess Consuela Banana-Hammock.

# Quiz Number 2
## Answers

1.  Ross sees her an thinks it's a sexual invitation.
2.  Due to a traumatic incident she had when she was four years old.
3.  Jack Geller.
4.  Erica.
5.  As he finds Ross and Rachel breaking up stressful which he feels is similar to his parents divorce.
6.  Phoebe.
7.  Neurosurgery.
8.  By racing wind up toys.
9.  Monica.
10. Personal Shopper.

# Quiz Number 3
## Answers

1. Duties.
2. The cranberry sauce.
3. As his shoes are too slippery.
4. A ugly fruit bowl.
5. Rachel's.
6. Phoebes sock-bunny.
7. Katie.
8. Richard Burke.
9. Do a dance routine they did in 8th grade.
10. As they win the "lightning round" of the trivia quiz against each other?

# QUIZ NUMBER 4
## ANSWERS

1. Leonard Haynes a director.
2. They are viewing an apartment Adjacent to Monica's and see the two having sex.
3. In the doorway of Central Perk coffee shop.
4. $300 million.
5. Th holiday Armadillo.
6. Phoebe.
7. Dina.
8. For Phoebe to take one of the kids off him to make it more manageable.
9. Her mother.
10. By moving in together.

# QUIZ NUMBER 5
## ANSWERS

1. Earl.
2. Gunther.
3. Her hygiene.
4. Porsche.
5. That it is used by students as a spot to makeout.
6. Janine.
7. Marta Kauffman.
8. Chandler.
9. Phoebe.
10. Frank Buffay.

# Quiz Number 6
## Answers

1. The Moon dance Diner.
2. Elizabeth.
3. His Barcalounger reclining chair.
4. Rachel.
5. for driving too slow.
6. Joey.
7. He falls down an elevator shaft.
8. A dog.
9. Greg and Jenny.
10. Joey.

# Quiz Number 7
## Answers

1. Central Perk.
2. As it's made of fur.
3. Kathy.
4. Slapped peoples buttocks.
5. She starts making loads of jam. She calls it the 'Jam Plan'.
6. How you doin'?
7. She went for lunch with Richard?
8. Monica.
9. A hairless cat.
10. Monica, Rachel and Phoebe.

# QUIZ NUMBER 8
## ANSWERS

1. 'Where?'.
2. As she was being tormented by her colleagues.
3. Phoebes date has shorts that everyone can see up, he also wears loose underwear letting people see his genitals.
4. He was an actor on a TV show.
5. Molly.
6. Someone at work takes his left over thanksgiving sandwich.
7. As Alice is 26 years older than frank.
8. Cujo.
9. As Emily doesn't want to sit anywhere Rachel sat.
10. As he finds out that its legal to smoke in offices with 15 people or less.

# QUIZ NUMBER 9
## ANSWERS

1. Soap Opera Digest.
2. Her grandma's chocolate chip recipe.
3. He keeps giving free coffee to all the prettygirls.
4. a penis.
5. As he reacts badly when he tells her she's pregnant.
6. Yemen.
7. Hootie and the Blowfish.
8. Emma Geller-Green.
9. Joey.
10. Chandler has to spend six hours locked in abox.

# QUIZ NUMBER 10
## ANSWERS

1. Aunt Iris Geller.
2. Rachel Green.
3. Jarvu's.
4. As he is in prison.
5. He died.
6. Bamboozled.
7. Tennis.
8. Her father.
9. Jill Goodacre.
10. Sandy.

# Quiz Number 11
## Answers

1. He says Rachel's name.
2. Marcel was taken during a break-in.
3. A new chick and duck.
4. Law&Order.
5. A 'tiny' T-shirt that Ross hasn't worn in 15 years. Rachel used it to sleep in.
6. Chandler.
7. A salt shaker.
8. Las Vegas.
9. Bloomingdale's.
10. Matthew Perry.

# Quiz Number 12
## Answers

1. A basket of mini-muffins.
2. Matt LeBlanc.
3. To try find her dad.
4. Science Boy.
5. Pink.
6. Rachel.
7. As he has so few people attending on hisside.
8. Aunt Sylvia.
9. erectile dysfunction.
10. Monica bumps his head while playingairplane.

# QUIZ NUMBER 13
## ANSWERS

1. His father.
2. As she makes out with one of her clients; named Rick.
3. He's trying to scare Chandler.
4. They went to go see the New York Rangers.
5. David.
6. Jogging.
7. Mac Machiavelli.
8. His Porsche.
9. Chandler.
10. As their friendship is too strong.

# Quiz Number 14
## Answers

1. A hypnosis tape.
2. In the basement of the apartment building.
3. He cant cry.
4. As they have been taking self-defenseclasses.
5. Nancy.
6. his dog Chappy.
7. A mix-tape.
8. Toby.
9. his butt.
10. Ross.

# QUIZ NUMBER 15
## ANSWERS

1. As he is scared Susan will turn Emily into a lesbian like she did to Carol.

2. Benjamin Hobart.

3. As Joey has given Monica money because her and Chandler were financially struggling and he wanted to hide this from Chandler.

4. For her to be their surrogate mother.

5. Ross singing 'Baby got back'.

6. Phoebe.

7. Wendy.

8. A photo frame.

9. She is using him as a baby sitter for her son.

10. Ross has sex with dinosaurs.

# QUIZ NUMBER 16
## ANSWERS

1. She's actually a hooker.
2. Fortunata Fashions.
3. New York Museum of Prehistoric History.
4. Doing an embarrassing dance and calling himself 'the man' and 'the love machine'.
5. By telling Rachel that the plane has a problem with the "left phalange". The guy sitting next to Rachel overhears this and freaks out causing the plane to be evacuated.
6. Westchester.
7. He finds a briefcase full of fossils.
8. Montreal.
9. 35 years.
10. Gunther confesses his love to Rachel and gets turned down.

# QUIZ NUMBER 17
## ANSWERS

1. As Richard doesn't want to have kids.
2. In a coma.
3. By pushing him into it.
4. Tommy.
5. On a bus.
6. Jack.
7. French.
8. Rachel.
9. Theodore Hannigan.
10. Ross.

# Quiz Number 18
## Answers

1. It's in Paris.
2. Mozzarella.
3. He gets her on Days Of Our Lives as an extra.
4. Julie.
5. Monica.
6. Spanish.
7. Russ.
8. Malcom.
9. Joey.
10. He promises to never smoke again.

# QUIZ NUMBER 19
## ANSWERS

1. Muriel.
2. As he finds out Ross has had three failed marriages.
3. Monica.
4. Tim.
5. Monica.
6. ornithophobia - fear of farm birds.
7. Chandler.
8. The babysitter Judy as she has a key.
9. She will die within a week.
10. Fun Bobby.

# QUIZ NUMBER 20
# ANSWERS

1.  Phoebe.
2.  Ross.
3.  Chandler.
4.  Janice.
5.  season 7.
6.  Bill.
7.  Porn
8.  Some candle holders.
9.  Kleinman's.
10. Lisa Kudrow.

# Quiz Number 21
## Answers

1. A Foosball table.
2. The I Hate Rachel Green Club.
3. on the street.
4. Eddie.
5. Two large leather reclining sofas as well as a large TV.
6. Barbados.
7. Cookies.
8. As he's a fan of her porn films.
9. A pigeon.
10. Phoebe.

# QUIZ NUMBER 22
## ANSWERS

1. Try's to smoke with them.
2. They went to go see a movie.
3. Janice Litman-Goralnik nee Hosenstein.
4. Rachel.
5. Duncan.
6. Long Island.
7. by doing a dramatic performance of Emma's favorite book.
8. Estelle Leonard his acting agent.
9. Her engagement ring from Barry.
10. Five years of the silent treatment.

# QUIZ NUMBER 23
## ANSWERS

1. Joey uses the wire from Phoebes bra to pick the lock.
2. Five.
3. Doctor.
4. a van.
5. Chandler.
6. Her former boss Mark.
7. Her ex-fiancé Barry.
8. Mary Angela.
9. Due to his anger issues.
10. 3, she has triplets.

# QUIZ NUMBER 24
## ANSWERS

1. Bagpipes.
2. He has to stop being friends with Rachel.
3. Carol Willick.
4. Phoebe.
5. Mr. Treeger.
6. Hire a personal assistant.
7. The gifts were intended to drive Rachel out of Joeys flat so that she would move back in with Phoebe.
8. Maria.
9. The Rockefeller Center.
10. Mokolate.

# QUIZ NUMBER 25
## ANSWERS

1. If she'd taken a job she was offered at 'Merrill Lynch'.
2. Ursula Buffay.
3. So he can marry Chandler and Monica.
4. Louis Vuitton.
5. Grabs his crotch.
6. Joey says she broke his golden rule of no sharing food.
7. As he's ugly and overweight.
8. One of the doctors that Rachel asks on a double date, named Dr. Michael Mitchell.
9. Tulsa Oklahoma.
10. Frank Jr.

# Quiz Number 26
## Answers

1. It was a video tape of Monica and Rachel getting ready for their senior prom.
2. Dr. Drake Ramoray.
3. San Diego Zoo.
4. As she catches Ross and Rachel kissing and wanted the day to be about her engagement not them getting back together.
5. He has to seep on the left side of the bed.
6. Jennifer Aniston.
7. Gunther.
8. A videotape marked 'Monica'.
9. As Monica has been illegally subletting a room in the flat to Rachel.
10. A dollhouse.

# QUIZ NUMBER 27
## ANSWERS

1. They break up.
2. As two of the cookbook pages were stuck together.
3. Huggsy.
4. Ross.
5. Vince.
6. Watches him sleep.
7. Central Perk.
8. Leslie.
9. Ben.
10. Mama's little Bakery.

# QUIZ NUMBER 28
## ANSWERS

1. They were friends in collage.
2. That she'll meet the man of her dreams soon.
3. Minsk.
4. She says that he forgot to take his Brain medicine meaning that women's names are interchangeable in his brain.
5. Ross and Rachel.
6. David Crane.
7. Bonnie.
8. He works as a Tour guide.
9. Estelle Leonard.
10. Ross.

# Quiz Number 29
## Answers

1. Charlie Wheeler.
2. Venereal Disease or VD.
3. That he can close down restaurants.
4. Al Pacino.
5. Sergei.
6. U2's With Or Without You.
7. As her shirt is see through.
8. 236.
9. Jill.
10. Free porn channel.

# Quiz Number 30
## Answers

1. That once they put Emma to sleep they had sex as Monica was ovulating.
2. Courtney Cox.
3. Monica is stopped by Rachel talking to her and Chandler discovers Mr. Waltham is giving guided tours of the house.
4. As they haven't played football since Monica broke Ross's nose while playing football when they were younger.
5. He was recording himself telling the 'Europe story' like Joey advised to get better at picking up girls.
6. Richard Burke's son Timothy.
7. Monica.
8. Gary Halvorson.
9. Chandler caught Kathy sleeping with Nick after they had a fight.
10. He unnecessarily intimidates a elderly couple who have accidentally sat in his and Ross' seats.

# QUIZ NUMBER 31
## ANSWERS

1. Gleeba.
2. It's a little baby Ross with his adult head.
3. season 6.
4. Rachels sister Amy.
5. Joey.
6. Phoebe wears a janitor's outfit with the nametag 'Ben' on it.
7. Joey.
8. Amanda.
9. By going down the fire escape.
10. Monica's grandmother.

# QUIZ NUMBER 32
## ANSWERS

1. Her boss Joanna.
2. Janice Litman-Goralnik nee Hosenstein.
3. inside a foosball table.
4. She just says "thank you!" in shock.
5. He buys the flat a new set of furniture, foosball table etc.
6. none.
7. An advertising company.
8. As PBS was the channel her mother watched sesame street on before committed suicide.
9. They were kissing.
10. Vermont.

# QUIZ NUMBER 33
## ANSWERS

1. Don.
2. As the groom was one of her former boyfriends.
3. A beauty contest.
4. Chandler and Joey's.
5. Playboy magazine.
6. Turns on and off Joey and Chandlers TV.
7. The shining.
8. Rachels hair iron.
9. Ross's grandmothers ring.
10. Ross.

# QUIZ NUMBER 34
## ANSWERS

1. As he knew that if Monica found out she'd enter them in doubles tournaments.
2. Chandler is viewing houses.
3. They bump into Richard who confesses his love to her.
4. As they are supposed to be biological twins for the experiment but are obviously not.
5. Carol Willick.
6. Eat thanksgiving dinner.
7. Ohio Cincinnati.
8. Kyle.
9. That he was adopted.
10. Ugly Naked Guy.

# QUIZ NUMBER 35
# ANSWERS

1. Ross.
2. Jason.
3. He was an Orthodontist.
4. As he could get fired if his bosses found out.
5. She writes him a naughty evaluation and without reading it he sends it to human resources.
6. Albert.
7. As every time she visits the dentist someone dies.
8. Dr. Wiener.
9. He slides his hand from her back to her butt.
10. Ross and her have sex.

# QUIZ NUMBER 36
## ANSWERS

1. Corn rows.
2. As while having her massage Monica started making sex noises.
3. She reads dirty books.
4. As he is afraid of them.
5. Chopsticks.
6. He is a drug addict who at the start of the date insults himself and starts to cry.
7. Ross sees him playing with a Barbie doll.
8. Mr. Zelner.
9. Phoebe's water breaks.
10. Sting.

# Quiz Number 37
## Answers

1. As he just got divorced.
2. That she's boring.
3. 55JIMBO.
4. A baby chick.
5. She used to make fun of him at school.
6. Erotic Writer.
7. Gingers wooden leg.
8. a human thumb.
9. Bob.
10. Vermont.

# Quiz Number 38
## Answers

1. Dr. Leonard Green.
2. Gucci.
3. Computerized Humanoid Electronically Enhanced Secret Enforcer.
4. They have a competition whereby they each have one more date with her with a $100 spending limit and see at the end of it who she likes more.
5. David Schwimmer.
6. He claims that Chandler is very gay.
7. Rosita.
8. sitting on the boat in the marina drinkingbeer.
9. Precious.
10. A Knicks game.

# QUIZ NUMBER 39
## ANSWERS

1.  The con's list said 'she's just a waiter'.
2.  Dutch.
3.  As she doesn't believe they'll go throughwith it.
4.  Julie Ross's new girlfriend.
5.  Gloria Tribbiani.
6.  Eat his sandwich.
7.  Pete.
8.  in the cake.
9.  A fireman.
10. Susan Bunch.

# QUIZ NUMBER 40
## ANSWERS

1. A tennis kit.
2. Crap Bag.
3. People mistake her collection tin as a trashcan.
4. Season 3.
5. Joey brings a girl home who sees the camera and thinks it was joeys intention for her.
6. The pipe holding open the door.
7. Joey.
8. It says he was killed by a blimp.
9. Gavin.
10. a Soapie Award.

# QUIZ NUMBER 41
## ANSWERS

1. Alessandro's.
2. Ross and Joey flip a coin.
3. He has a brain transplant with a woman.
4. They were best friends in high school.
5. Brenda.
6. In a cleaning closet.
7. Monica's boyfriend Pete.
8. A set of encyclopedia's.
9. 10.
10. Wear her underwear during the date.

# QUIZ NUMBER 42
## ANSWERS

1. Central Perk.
2. As he finds out that when Monica knocked on the apartment when she and Chandler met, Monica was trying to sleep with .Joey but he wasn't in.
3. As she's unhappy with the cleanliness of the rooms.
4. As she is pregnant and cannot fly.
5. Julio.
6. A top hat.
7. In Greenwich Village, it's also in the same apartment block as Monica's apartment.
8. Their wedding china.
9. Kidney Stones.
10. Days of our Lives had a float at the thanksgiving day parade and he was supposed to attend.

# QUIZ NUMBER 43
## ANSWERS

1. the game Ms. Pac-Man.
2. Chick Jr. and Duck Jr.
3. 22nd September 1994.
4. She was hit by a cab and died before submitting any paperwork regarding the promotion.
5. By using silly putty.
6. The condom company.
7. 6th May 2004.
8. He wants her to be the head chef of his new restaurant.
9. Janice Litman-Goralnik nee Hosenstein.
10. As Chandler hates thanksgiving food and he wont eat the leftovers.

# QUIZ NUMBER 44
## ANSWERS

1. The infamous Princess Leia Return of the Jedi scene.
2. Lowell.
3. As is family have a history of divorces and he is scared of the same happening and hurting Monica.
4. The Velveteen Rabbit.
5. Chandlers smile makes him look like ahyena.
6. He picks up a bag that a girl dropped, to thank him she gives him a kiss. This is actually Ross' new girlfriend but Rachel is unaware.
7. Tag Jones.
8. Swing Kings.
9. Laura.
10. She says that 'Monica talks very loud for a small person'.

# QUIZ NUMBER 45
## ANSWERS

1. Erica.
2. An apothecary table.
3. Mr. Heckles.
4. Ross.
5. homemade free candy
6. She committed suicide.
7. Marcel.
8. Cups.
9. Joey.
10. Donate it to charity.